G000134448

Black's Picture Sports

Judo

Black's Picture Sports
Judo

Sports Illustrated · Revised by

Kevin Murphy

Adam and Charles Black · London

Reprinted 1984
First published 1980 by
A & C Black (Publishers) Ltd, 35 Bedford Row
London WC1R 4JH

ISBN 0-7136-2002-1
Authorised British edition

Originally published in the United States of America
by J B Lippincott Company as *Sports Illustrated Judo*
by Paul Stewart and the Editors of *Sports Illustrated*.

Murphy, Kevin
Judo. – British ed. – (Black's picture sports).
1. Judo
I. Title II. Stewart, Paul
III. 'Sports illustrated' judo
796.8'152 GV1114
ISBN 0-7136-2002-1

Cover photo by David Finch
Photographs by Peter Medley and Joan Murphy
The team in the photographs consists of Kevin Murphy (6th Dan), Joan Murphy (4th Dan), Peter Hare (2nd Dan), Martin Smithson (3rd Kyu) and Ian Smith (2nd Kyu).

Filmset and printed in Great Britain by
BAS Printers Limited, Over Wallop, Hampshire.

Contents

JUDO RANKS

Colours indicate belts worn. The junior system of grading is Ko-Kyu; the senior Kyu and the black belts are Dans.

JUNIOR

1st Ko-Kyu (White)
2nd Ko-Kyu (Yellow)
3rd Ko-Kyu (Orange)
4th Ko-Kyu (Green)
5th Ko-Kyu (Blue)
6th Ko-Kyu (Brown)

(3 grades at each colour division: 18 grades in all.)

SENIOR

6th Kyu (White)
5th Kyu (Yellow)
4th Kyu (Orange)
3rd Kyu (Green)
2nd Kyu (Blue)
1st Kyu (Brown)

BLACK BELT RANKS

1st Shodan
2nd Nidan
3rd Sandan
4th Yodan*
5th Godan
6th Rokudan
7th Shichidan
8th Hachidan
9th Kudan
10th Judan

*Advanced grades start here.

1 Introduction

THE JAPANESE HERITAGE OF JUDO

Judo is a remnant of ancient Japan, a society where courtesy and respect for elders was important, and there was a strong feeling for the ceremonious act.

At the time when Japan was a feudal society, there were schools for learning how to battle with swords, bows and arrows, clubs, spears and with the bare hands. *Jujitsu* means 'the art of fighting', and in ancient Japan it had been developed into a lethal science. But as Japan entered modern times, the ancient martial arts began to disappear slowly, and new weapons were introduced.

However, in 1882, a man called Jigora Kano decided to re-think the techniques of *jujitsu*. He removed its dangerous elements, such as the foot and hand strikes. Kano called his new sport judo, which means 'the gentle way'. To many people, though, this would seem an obvious contradiction. How can such a sport be considered gentle?

Kano's attitude to the new sport can be understood from the passage below:

> let us suppose that we estimate the strength of man in units of one. Let us say that the strength of a man standing in front of me is represented by ten units, whereas my strength, less than his, is represented by seven units. Now, if he pushes me with all his force I shall certainly be pushed back or thrown down, even if I use all my strength against his . . . . But if, instead of opposing him, I were to give way to his strength by withdrawing my body just as much as he had

pushed, taking care at the same time to keep my balance, then he would naturally lean forward and thus lose his balance.

In this new position, he may have become so weak (not in actual physical strength, but because of his awkward position) as to have his strength represented for the moment by only three units, instead of his normal ten units. But meanwhile, by keeping my balance, I retain my full strength, as originally represented by seven units. Here then, I am momentarily in a superior position, and can defeat my opponent by using only half my strength, that is half of my seven units, or three and one-half, against his three. This leaves one-half of my strength available for any purpose. Now if I had greater strength than my opponent I could of course push him back. But even if I wished to push him back and had the power to do so, it would still be better for me first to give way, because by doing so I would have greatly economised my energy and exhausted my opponent's.

That passage reveals the true secret of all techniques of judo; the idea is to manoeuvre a stronger opponent into a position where he cannot use his full strength against you and where you may use your full strength to greater advantage.

In judo, you must learn to capitalise on your opponent's weaknesses. If he or she is too tall, he will probably be slower than you. You'll also learn to capitalise on an opponent's emotions. If a player rushes at you too aggressively, you will learn the moves which will both blunt his attack and bring about his defeat. Judo requires great finesse, co-ordination of the entire body, concentration of thought and, equally, concentration of power. Often a tiny thing can mean success or failure for a judo player. Your arms must push or pull, your legs must sweep and chop, and your head must guide all your movements so that you act quickly, decisively and with precision. Only when all these are brought together effectively will a judo player succeed. This book is intended to guide you as rapidly as possible to a reasonable standard of competitive judo. Once you have learnt *how* to practise, proficiency will come with the amount of practice you do. Of course, you only get out of a sport what you are prepared to put in – but once you have begun you are on the right road towards excellence in your chosen field.

JUDO IN BRITAIN

It is generally accepted that judo came to Britain at the end of the nineteenth century – certainly judo/jujitsu had arrived in 1889 when Yuko Tani toured the music halls challenging the audience to do combat with him. While Yukio Tani was touring the halls, another Japanese expert had arrived, 'Raku' Uyenishi, the jujitsu champion of the world, and he set up studios in London, Liverpool and Birmingham, raising a great deal of interest in the sport.

In 1918, Gunji Koizumi opened a club called 'The Budokwai', and he was largely responsible for judo's development as a sport during the 1920s and 30s. However, at this time, English judo experts were beginning to be recognised; probably the first genuine English 'Master' was E J Harrison, followed later by Trevor Leggatt. However, not much was known about judo in the late 1940s – the sport was still shrouded in mystery and misguided people talked knowledgeably about touching nerve points and sending people flying through the air!

Two Japanese masters were prominent in the 1950s – Kenshiro Abbe, 8th Dan, and Matsutaro O'Tani. Kenshiro Abbe brought a new and exciting dimension to judo, and attracted a great deal of attention. O'Tani, on the other hand, was a less sensational figure, and had been a quiet influence on judo's development in Britain since the 1930s. O'Tani's emphasis on tradition, courtesy and friendliness is still with us, and, we hope, always will be.

During the 1950s, many British born judo Masters came into their own, and this really began to capture the imagination of judo followers in England. Suddenly, everyone was talking of the British Masters – Geoff Gleeson, Pat Butler, Tony Sweeney, Frank Ryder, Jim Cooney, to name but a few. And in 1964, judo became an Olympic sport, with all the international interest that such tournaments excite.

Now we are in the 1980s and judo has a tradition to look back on, and there are instructors still teaching with twenty five to fifty years of experience of the sport to pass on to their students. Recently, the organisation of championships has improved, and they are rather less of a scramble than they used to be. Reflecting this, teachers are now required to give more time to efficient organisation of the sport. Also, the average judo instructor is now learning more about physical fitness, as part of his/her judo training programme.

Most club coaches are now reasonably good organisers, proficient referees and are way above average physical educationalists, which can only be of advantage to the student. Judo is now a highly organised and contested force in the sporting world – and you are about to take your first steps to become part of it.

GETTING STARTED

Judo is now practised in schools, youth clubs and in evening classes. Details of evening classes can be obtained from your local Further Education authorities, and you can also find out about what classes are available from your local library.

There are many excellent judo clubs run privately by highly qualified instructors who, for a variety of reasons, prefer not to be part of the Further Education system. These private clubs are usually run on a semi-professional basis by black belt judo teachers, and are often open all the year round – there are some clubs that even have sessions on Christmas Day! These semi-professional clubs often meet in village or church halls on one or more nights a week according to the demand, and the students share the work (laying out judo mats, sweeping up and so on) and the expense of the hall. Students in these clubs usually work together very happily, and develop a tremendous loyalty to their club and instructor (*sensei*).

Also, many large factories have their own sports club, which may often organise judo sessions, though of course these may only be open to the firm's work force.

In Great Britain, there are many judo organisations you

can get in touch with if you have difficulty in finding a club in your area, or if you have more general questions. Addresses of some of the most important associations are listed on p. 88.

2 Basic Techniques

WHAT TO EXPECT

First you must learn the terminology of the sport. You may find it difficult at first to remember the Japanese words, but they will soon become familiar. A glossary of terms most commonly used is found on pp. 90 and 91 of this book.

You will learn in a *dojo*, meaning the studio or gym. The *sensei* is your instructor. The clothing you wear, the tunic and loose trousers of heavy cotton, is called a *gi*.

It is important that you understand the terms *tori* and *uke*. *Tori* is the player who performs the throw, and *uke* is the player who is thrown. In groundwork, *tori* is the player who performs the hold, lock or choke, *uke* being the player usually 'underneath' who succumbs to *tori*'s hold, lock or choke. Remember, *tori* is the one who does, and *uke* is the one it is done to. These terms are used in describing what is happening in the illustrations throughout this book.

The next thing you'll learn is how significant courtesy is in judo. The very fact that a bow, or *rei* is important, says something about the nature of the sport. This bow indicates the physical courtesy and respect you have towards another student, an opponent, or the *sensei*. You bow when you enter the *dojo*, to show respect for this learning place. The class starts with a bow, and in *randori* (that is, fighting practice), you must bow before and after each match. The class ends with a bow, too. It is important to show respect towards other people in judo, for ultimately this disciplined courtesy helps you to have control of your emotions. At one moment,

Figure 1. In a standing bow, *tachi rei*, a judo player places his arms at his sides and bows from the waist, slowly and with gentleness.

Figure 2. In a kneeling bow, *za rei*, the judo player starts by kneeling and then crossing his feet. Next, he places his palms on his thighs, with his knees slightly spread. Now he bends downwards, placing his palms on the mat in front of his knees; his elbows are out and forwards of his body.

you may fight aggressively and vigorously and in the next moment help another student interested in learning a throw.

After the *rei*, you'll immediately go into warming up exercises, first stretching the back, hands, legs, and neck.

Loosening and stretching these muscles is important, as it helps prevent injuries. You'll encounter enormous stresses and strains in judo and your muscles, if properly warmed up, will be that much more resilient.

WARMING UP

Warming up routines are many and varied, but here is a good ten minutes warming up session that will prepare you for practice.

Exercise 1	two minutes jogging, with long and short strides.
Exercise 2	one minute of trunk bends, to the front, rear and side.
Exercise 3	thirty seconds of squats.
Exercise 4	to develop the abdomen, do sit ups. Try a minimum of ten repeats, every thirty seconds.
Exercise 5	Tense your arm muscles by doing a minimum of ten press ups in thirty seconds (or as many as you can manage). Then relax the tensed muscles by standing, bending from the waist and rotating the arms rapidly in a very relaxed circular motion.
Exercise 6	Try head presses (bridging), a minimum of ten every thirty seconds (again, as many as you can manage). Then relax by rotating the head slowly in circular motion.
Exercise 7	Do high jumps, bringing the knees close to the chest, ten every thirty seconds. Relax by kicking the heels towards the floor.
Exercise 8	You can try Taiotoshi exercises to stretch and strengthen the back, groin and leg muscles; all stretching exercises are highly beneficial for judo practice and should always be practised to left and right.
Exercise 9	Hand grip strengthening exercises; hold your arms at full stretch in front of you. Open and stretch your fingers then tightly clench your fist. Repeat this twenty times. Do more as the exercise becomes easy. Relax by bending the

Figure 3. Taiotoshi exercises to left and right.

Side trunk bending to to be done left and right; d shows bridging or the head press.

trunk and allowing your arms to hang loosely. Then rotate your arms.

Exercise 10 Lie down flat on your back with your arms stretched above your head. Raise your legs and the trunk of your body to form a V shape and touch your toes with your hands. Return to starting position and repeat ten times.

It is important after every exercise creating muscular tension to relax the muscles before starting the next exercise.

WEIGHT LIFTING

For the player who has developed to normal fitness level, light weight training can be very beneficial; however, do not be tempted to start any weight training until the normal exercise routine given above becomes too easy for you.

Of course, you will realise in your early lessons that weight lifting is a major part of judo! You will regularly be lifting the weight of your opponent in practice, as all throwing actions demand at some point the ability to lift, or partly lift, your opponent, sometimes with the hips, sometimes with the hands and sometimes with the legs, and often with a combination of all three. The development of these lifts is called *uchikomi*, meaning 'repetitive practice'. *Uchikomi* is the truest weight lifting programme for the judo player, as the lines of the muscles in use during a throwing action are fully worked on during *uchikomi* practice, with the body of a fellow player being used as the weight. *Uchikomi* is often referred to as 'standing practice', as one player stands and allows their partner to enter into the required throwing position, lifting their body weight and putting them down on their feet without actually throwing them.

It is essential that when practising *uchikomi* you concentrate on moving accurately into a position where you can lift the opponent; and when you have arrived at the correct position from which to lift, carry out that lift. It is not enough just to arrive at a lifting position and move out without a lift having taken place, for the exercise will not then be of any benefit. Once an accurate lifting position is established, speed and strength of movement will develop automatically with regular practice. Remember the word *uchikomi*, and if you always relate it to accuracy of lifting movements you will find yourself a more successful judo player.

HOW TO FALL

Ukemi, or falling practice, is the first and one of the most important areas of study, since falling is a major part of judo. You'll be thrown as often as you throw somebody else, and learning how to fall can prevent injuries; you will also gain confidence in your ability to fall, which comes only with practice.

It is a good idea to practise falling at every lesson. Learn the essential techniques and practise them over and over again, until they are automatic reflexes. The first essential is to always tuck your chin in, which helps to prevent any shock to the back of your head when you land on your back. The second essential is always to try and spread the shock of the impact over as large an area of your body as possible. Land on your back if you can and develop the habit of always slapping the mat. Doing these things can be difficult at first, but if you practise falling again and again, the proper fall will become instinctive and easy.

Sometimes you will find it far better to let yourself be thrown when your cause is lost than to keep fighting. If you don't fall so as to land safely on your back, you may land on your knees, which are far more vulnerable to injury.

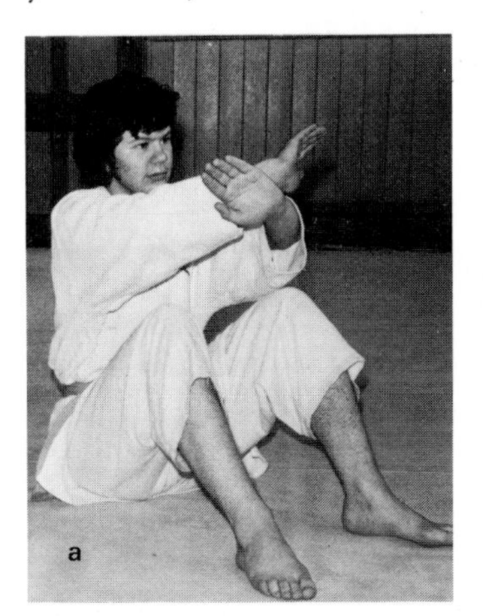

Figure 4. To fall from a sitting position, raise your arms and start to fall back. Just as your back is about to hit it, slap the mat hard with both arms. This helps break your fall. Remember to keep your chin tucked in. Practise this fall from a standing position and a squatting position.

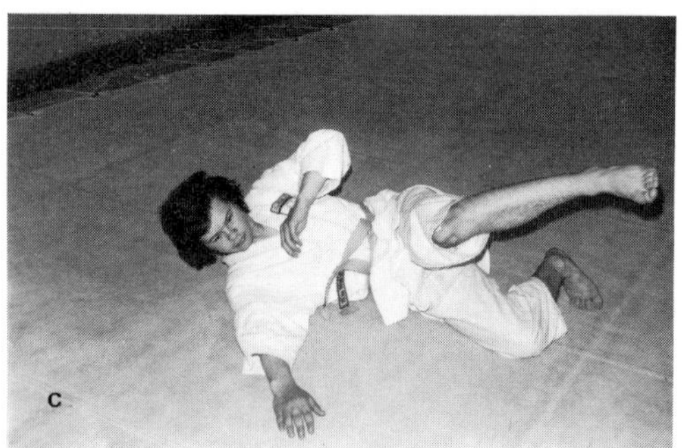

Figure 5. a, b and c: to fall sideways, like on your back, raise your legs and roll to one side. Slap the mat on the side you are turning to. Keep your chin tucked in on this fall too, to protect your head and neck. Now do the same thing on the other side. Practise this fall as much as possible because you will be thrown this way hundreds of times. Always keep your arms and body relaxed while breakfalling and learn to strike the *tatami* with the whole of your arms from the hand to the shoulder.

BREAKFALLS

The whole object of a 'breakfall' is to soften the impact of landing from a fall, slowing down the rate of descent of the falling body, by forcibly striking the *tatami* (the mat) with one or both arms a fraction of a second before the rest of the body accepts the impact of the fall. If the breakfall is timed and executed correctly the trunk of the body will stop falling at the moment your arms strike the *tatami*. From this 'stopped' position, the body will then recommence its downward flight from between three and four inches above the *tatami*, so no matter how high the throw and no matter how forcibly you have been thrown, providing you have executed a good breakfalling action, the body landing will always be the same; from an arrested position about three or four inches above the mat.

As you can imagine, it is not possible to hurt yourself falling onto a rubber mat or straw *tatami* from three or four inches – but the movement requires great attention until you have perfected it. Figures 4 and 5 illustrate different kinds of breakfalls, and show you how to execute them.

Chugari (Rolling Breakfall) From certain throws, the body will move horizontally to the mat surface. This requires a different kind of falling action, known as the 'rolling breakfall'. Any round object rolling along a flat surface will lose momentum and stop. Your body must become that round object as soon as contact with the *tatami* is made, allowing the force of the throw to expend itself with your rolling action. Skilled players often roll to their feet and regain balance at a standing position.

HOW TO STAND

It is very important that you have a comfortable stance. Your body should be relaxed but not limp. You must be able to move quickly and strongly from your stance.

For an attacking stance, your feet should be slightly apart and your hands at your sides. Your posture, in effect, is erect. You can lead slightly with your right or left foot if it is more

Figure 6. *Chugari* – forward roll.
Left to right: to tumble forward in the judo roll, place your hands on the side of your lead foot. Tuck the lead shoulder in to prevent it from hitting the mat. Push with your feet and roll. Again, keep your chin tucked in. As you start to land on your back, slap the mat with your arm as hard as you can to help you rise.

comfortable for you, or you know it to be advantageous for you. It is less tiring to stand in this natural posture, and it is a remarkably effective position from which to apply throws. The Japanese term for attacking stance is *shizen tai*.

In defending against an opponent's throw, spread your feet wider, bend your knees and lower your body. From this lower position it is easier to resist. To counter a sweeping hip throw (see p. 52) sink lower and turn your hip against your opponent. However, you should also remember that you do not win a match on defensive play alone; this deep defensive stance puts you into an awkward offensive posture. It is hard to execute throws from this position. The Japanese for this position is *jigo tai* (see page 88).

HOW TO MOVE

It is unwise to walk naturally across the mat – instead, move your body across it with short, sliding steps. Never cross your feet as you move, for that would make it relatively easy for an opponent to apply a foot sweep against you (see p. 42). Your balance must be low; to help with this, keeping

your feet on the mat as long as you can will certainly help you defend against throws.

YOUR GRIP

Many techniques involve the use of the *gi*. As you grip your opponent's *gi*, you should grip strongly, but not so strongly as to tire your arms and hand. For a moment, pretend you are gripping a screwdriver. You will notice you grip with the three smaller fingers, and your thumb and index fingers are used as guides. That's precisely the way you grip the lapel of your opponent's *gi*. The thumb and index finger should remain loose, and the other three tight.

Figure 7. *Shizen tai. a* shows the ideal position for offensive judo. The players are relaxed but ready to spring into action. In *b*, you see the perfect defensive position in judo. By bending your knees and placing your feet further apart, you are lowering your centre of gravity. It will be hard for anyone to penetrate your defence. However, this stance has obvious shortcomings, as it is not an effective way to start an attack of your own.

In a normal grip, you will grip your opponent's left lapel with your right hand, keeping your upper arm close to your body. Your left hand grips his right sleeve, somewhere around the elbow. Your grip must be comfortable to you – like the stance, it depends on personal preference. If you play a smaller person, you may find it more comfortable to grip the back of his *gi*. For your own protection, you may not grip the end of your opponent's sleeve or trousers. It would be easy for him to twist and perhaps injure your hand. All grips must be above the waistline of the jacket.

UCHIKOMI (PRACTICE FOR TECHNIQUE)

We have already discussed *uchikomi* in relation to practising lifting movements – in addition, during this part of the lesson (which follows the warming up exercises) you will be expected to practise your throws, hold-downs and chokes. The instructor usually moves from person to person, advising each one how to throw better. Generally, he

Figure 8. A natural hold.

matches you with someone of equivalent size. You exchange throws with your partner, working on timing, footwork, and grips.

Ne waza (see page 88), or fighting on the ground, is a large part of the sport, and includes an enormous variety of hold-downs, armlocks, and choking techniques. Typical groundwork exercises are as follows: partners sit back to back, and at the count of three each whirls round and tries to immobilise the other with an armlock or choke him into submission. You might also be allowed to put a hold-down on an opponent which he will try to break. All groundwork exercises build stamina and strength. Hold-down and choking techniques are discussed in chapters 4 and 5.

RANDORI (FIGHTING PRACTICE)

The last part of a lesson is *randori*, or fighting practice. Now you will be expected to apply your knowledge of judo against an opponent. The most common mistake is to try to battle too hard. The *randori* is practice; the *shiai*, described on p. 26, is the contest. If you are going to improve your judo, you must not be afraid of trying new and more difficult techniques, even if you will be effectively countered or perhaps thrown to the mat. You must accept that you will be thrown, probably many times.

You must practise your throws by learning to vary your attack, and trying to take advantage of a flaw in your opponent's defence. Many players, perhaps afraid of losing face in practice, simply go into a defensive crouch. It may be hard to throw them from this position, of course, but it is equally hard for them to throw an opponent.

Your progress in judo will depend on how well and how thoroughly you use *randori*. Practise with as many different players, big and small, as you can in the course of *randori*. You will find that each judo player has a different style, and it becomes a challenge to outwit him strategically.

SHIAI (CONTEST)

The ultimate test of your skill is, of course, against an opponent in an actual contest. Depending on the level of the competition senior contests last from between three to twenty minutes. The *tatami* in national competitions is normally 30′ × 30′, with a 6′ safety area surrounding the competition area. Contests are controlled by a referee and two corner judges, the corner judges being fully qualified referees in their own right.

The object of a match is to defeat your opponent by an *ippon*, the value of an *ippon* being ten points. You can score an *ippon* with one clean throw, which terminates the contest in your favour. If the throw is not good enough, you might get a near point or *waza ari* with a scoring value of seven points. Two *waza ari* by the same player would finish off the bout, with the referee calling *waza-ari-awasete-ni-ippon*, which means two near points equalling one *ippon*, which terminates the contest in the favour of that player. *Waza ari* is the only judo score that can accumulate to terminate a contest; the other judo scores of *yuko* (five points) and *koka* (three points) are non-accumulative. If one player scores thirty *kokas* and another only fifteen, the player with thirty will win; however, should a player gain any number of *kokas* and his opponent gain just one *yuko*, with the higher scoring value of five points, the player gaining the *yuko* would be declared the winner as he would have shown greater technical skill.

Skill, then, is the overriding and determining factor of all judo techniques, for the more skilful your technique the higher the points you will gain. It is clear that a player should develop the skill to bring about an *ippon* to terminate the contest with the full and finalising score of ten points. You must not be content with continuously 'knocking' someone down for *kokas*, only to be beaten by a better single score of *yuko*, *waza ari* or *ippon*.

You can also win a contest by a hold-down. In a hold-down you win by controlling your opponent for thirty seconds in a choke or armlock, which will award you an *ippon*. If you maintain a hold-down for fifteen seconds, you are awarded a *koka*, for twenty seconds you are awarded a *yuko*, and for twenty-five seconds you gain a *waza ari* (see page 88).

Figure 9. Children may enter judo contests when they are five years old. Here you see two nine year old boys in *shiai.*

Figure 10. Full contest mats (*tatami*) in use at Crystal Palace National Sports Centre.

Ippon may also be scored by gaining a submission from your opponent from a strangle/choke or armlock. The defeated player submits by tapping the mat, or his opponent's body or by calling '*mattai*' (I am beaten).

Penalties Penalties may be given against a player who knowingly or unknowingly breaks the rules of judo competition. The penalties depend on the severity of the infringement, and are as follows:

Shido	3 points default
Chui	5 points default
Keikoku	7 points default
Hansoko make	10 (disqualification)

The rules of judo do not allow for the same penalty to be given more than once; this means that a player having the minor infringement of *shido* (3 points) who commits some other minor infringement is penalised more seriously a second time, and would gain a penalty of *chui* for the next mistake. That player would then have a total of five points in default. Should that player then make another mistake and be penalised again, he would have a penalty of seven points, a *kei koku*. At this stage, the only way the player thus penalised could win the contest would be by scoring *ippon* over his opponent – and he could lose the contest by committing yet another minor fault and being disqualified.

A good judo coach will always ensure that his pupils become aware of the rules of judo at a very early stage in their training. Ignorance of the rules is no excuse in a judo competition, so be sure that you know them well.

Do remember that the rules of judo are for the benefit and safety of all players, and the referee only penalises a contestant so that the sport can be practised with the utmost safety.

3 Throwing Techniques (Nage Waza)

A well executed judo throw is put together with accurate timing and great precision. You step in, pivot and pull your opponent onto your hips, sweeping him off his feet and down on the mat with your legs. All this sounds deceptively simple, of course; before you can actually throw a player you need to know how to stand, how to move on the mat, how to grip your opponent's *gi*, how to break his balance, and finally, how to actually get him off his feet and onto his back.

Strategically, you can take advantage of a sudden lunge by your opponent. As he lunges, he'll be vulnerable to an attack, since he'll be off balance and unable to retaliate with his full strength. You'll discover the kinds of throws to use in such situations.

Alternatively, you can start the action, by pushing your opponent hard. He may push back just as hard, and if he does, he may be opening himself up to attack. You will learn by experience how the push-pull principle works. If you pull someone onto your back, you'll be pushing against his legs. The object in setting up the opening position for a throw is to put your opponent on a horizontal plane. If you pull his torso to one side, you'll sweep his legs to the other. With a large number of throws the laws of mechanics operate so clearly that you may understand the art of throwing better if you think of it in these terms.

In many throws, the primary object is to get under your opponent, pulling him off his feet and onto your hip, so that you can throw him off that hip or off your back. Think of your hip or back as a lever; if you get under your opponent far enough, you won't need much force to throw him to the mat. But if you don't get deep enough, you may not be able to throw him at all.

BREAKING YOUR OPPONENT'S BALANCE (KUZUSHI)

This is the key to a throw in judo. The successful player is one who understands how to manipulate his opponent into breaking his natural balance.

If your opponent's weight is on his heels, he cannot attack you, and he is also susceptible to an attack from you. If his weight is on his toes, he has lost the offensive, however temporarily and is again made vulnerable.

You can break your opponent's balance in a number of directions if you push or pull him. You can push him quickly, and, if he resists, pull him forwards on his toes and execute a throw. Or, you can pull him first and as he resists your pull by putting his weight on his heels, push him.

Always throw a player in the direction in which he is moving. If a player always leans forwards, throw him forwards; you will not be able to throw him backwards. You will probably find that your opponent is most vulnerable to attack when he is stepping forwards or backwards, pivoting to his right or left at the split second before he tries to throw you. Remember then: *to achieve a throw you must position your opponent so that you are able to take away his last remaining point of balance.* Until the last point of balance has been taken away, your opponent is still standing, and anyone standing must have some degree of balance enabling him to resist.

OSOTO GARI (MAJOR OUTER REAPING)

Of all the judo throws, *osoto gari* is the easiest to learn and execute. Properly done, it is a devastatingly powerful throw. Even when it isn't executed correctly, however, a judo player can make *osoto gari* work for him.

The strategy is really quite simple; try to push your opponent's weight onto one foot, and then sweep that leg

Figure 12. *Osoto gari* (major outer reaping)

In this sequence, as *tori* brings her right leg down and into her opponent's leg, her right arm suddenly reverses the pressure. Instead of pulling her opponent into her, she pushes back and up against her opponent's neck.

As *tori* brings her right leg down, she points her foot. This increases the downward momentum of her leg. As her thigh hits the back of her opponent's thigh, *tori*'s forehead falls straight at the mat. All of her power is channelled into the leg sweep and the arm push, all of which will send her opponent onto the horizontal plane and crashing to the mat.

Because the opponent is swept so cleanly off her one foot, she simply cannot resist. But in many cases, your opponent will be able to block your first effort. If so, relax your pressure for a fraction of a second; your opponent may be fooled into thinking you've given up. Then try another *osoto gari.* It usually works if you put enough power into it.

Figure 11. The last remaining point of balance taken. To gain an *ippon* both of your opponent's feet must lift clear of the *tatami*. Then you must land your opponent mainly on his/her back with enough force to warrant an *ippon*.

out from under him, pushing him backwards at the same time. As you'll see on the following pages, *osoto gari* illustrates three basic concepts of judo – opportunity, anticipation and co-ordination.

Opportunity If you are using *osoto gari* to throw an opponent, you must be sure you can reach the target, which is his leg. If your opponent consistently leads with his right foot, he may be vulnerable to *osoto gari*. As you play other students in *randori* and *shiai*, you'll spot many opportunities to use the throw, and you should take advantage of them.

As you compete in higher ranks, however, you will have to create your own opportunity. In *osoto gari*, if you pull your opponent to the left, he'll resist, possibly even putting more weight on his right foot. Use that moment to strike.

Anticipation Once you've taken advantage of, or created your own opportunity, timing becomes the essential factor. You should try to throw your opponent the instant before he starts a throw, or starts to defend himself against a 'bluff' throw of yours. In this way, judo becomes much like a chess game in which you try to think out your opponent's strategy and then take advantage of it. For example, imagine that your right foot is vulnerable for an *osoto gari*. Suddenly you realise that your opponent has spotted this opening, and you know instinctively that he is coming at you with an *osoto gari*. If it looks like being a weak throw, you could counter it with a more powerful *osoto gari* of your own. Or, if he's powerful at this technique, you should attempt another throw.

Co-ordination Each judo throw is carefully co-ordinated, and all parts of the body must act in unison. If your leg sweeps an opponent's leg out from under him, as in *osoto gari*, then your arms push his torso backwards. As was emphasised before, the aim is to put your opponent on a horizontal plane so that he may fall as quickly as possible. As you sweep his feet to one side or another, pull his body the other way.

Figure 13. *Ouchi gari* (major inner reaping).
a. *Tori* places his foot in between his opponent's legs moving it in a circular motion to hook the back of his opponent's knee. *Tori* points his toes so that the back of his heel forms a hook and locks his foot successfully in an *ouchi gari*.
b. *Tori* spots an opportunity for *ouchi gari*. His opponent is not in a secure defensive stance. He is standing in too erect a posture, and is leaving himself open for a leg throw. To create an even better opening, *tori* pulls his opponent's right sleeve forwards, and pushes his left lapel. He has made his opponent wonder what *tori* is going to do. The opponent decides to resist and brings his left foot forwards, right into *tori*'s trap.
c. *Tori*'s right hand, with a firm grip, holds onto his opponent's left lapel and pushes him back and to the left. *Tori*'s left hand pushes his opponent in that same direction.

OUCHI GARI (MAJOR INNER REAPING)

Ouchi gari, like *osoto gari*, is a good leg throw to master when you begin, as it is a simple and effective move. The aim is to hook the inside of your opponent's leg and pull that leg towards you. As you do this, you'll push his torso back, again attempting to put your opponent on the horizontal plane.

The kind of mistake you are likely to make is not getting your opponent's leg hooked sufficiently hard, or in trying to hook your opponent's leg you may forget to push against his torso.

It may be that a player will succeed with the hooking movement, exert a powerful push and yet completely

d and e. The manoeuvre is completed as *tori* follows with the torso push and the leg hook. There is no way the falling player can resist this effective throw now.

d

e

abandon the move when the opponent puts up resistance. An experienced player, however, will not give up, but continue to hook and push to try and keep driving his opponent back across the mat. Essentially, you'll be hopping on one foot, and your opponent will be forced into hopping backwards on one foot while your foot will keep his other foot trapped in the hooking motion. As long as you maintain the driving pressure, you will maintain your equilibrium, but your opponent may very well fall.

HIZA GURUMA (KNEE WHEEL)

Hiza guruma is a sudden move that depends almost completely on speed for its effectiveness. It is valuable to learn this move as soon as possible and continue to practise it at every session. *Hiza guruma* startles opponents and can 'loosen' an opponent up so that you can follow up with a strong second throw.

KOSHI GURUMA (LOIN WHEEL)

If you are faced with a taller opponent, you might decide to attack with *koshi guruma*, a fast, powerful hip throw. Like all hip throws, it requires the same footwork, enabling you to get to the position 'inside' your opponent from which you can throw him most effectively. Practise those steps as often as you can. First, step inside and slightly ahead of your opponent's right foot, pivot with that foot and bring your left foot back inside your opponent's legs.

Figure 14. *Hiza garuma* (knee wheel).
a. This is the critical point of *hiza garuma*. You should slap the sole of your striking foot against your opponent's kneecap. You'll see how *tori* almost cradles his opponent's kneecap with the sole of his foot. He is delivering the maximum slap against that vulnerable spot.
b. *Tori* steps in and to the side with his left foot, pivoting when necessary to provide a base from which to strike out with his right foot.

Figure 15. *Koshi guruma (loin wheel).*
a. Armed with a good grip, *tori* steps forward with his right foot.
b. With his right foot in a pivoting position, *tori* pulls hard on his opponent's right sleeve to throw him off balance. With his right hand, he is going deep behind his opponent's neck.

c. As he pivots, *tori*'s right foot sweeps out in a straight line. The sole of his right foot slaps against his opponent's left kneecap. You will see how *tori*'s use of his arms strengthens the force of his *hiza garuma*. In a lifting, pulling movement, he seeks to shift his opponent's weight onto that leg under attack.
d. *Tori* has now forced his opponent onto the one foot. In effect, his opponent's body is going to revolve around his left kneecap. *Tori* uses his arms as if he were turning the steering wheel of a car.

c. With a good inside position, *tori* now has it all together: low hip position to give him plenty of lifting power, a good grip around his opponent's neck for pulling him onto his hip. *Tori*'s left arm helps to unbalance his opponent, pulling him ahead and forwards.
d. Here *tori* has his opponent 'floating' on his hip, ready to throw him down on the mat.

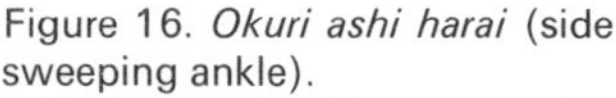

Figure 16. *Okuri ashi harai* (side sweeping ankle).
a. *Tori* is creating his opportunity, moving his opponent from side to side, from front to back. If his opponent is wary of leaning too much in one direction, *tori* has a chance of helping him go in that direction with an immediate *okuri ashi harai*. Or, if *tori* pushes his opponent hard into one direction, he can strike the split second before his opponent counters with a push back.

b. *Tori* strikes with the sole of his foot against a point just below his opponent's ankle bone. (When you are performing this throw, concentrate on keeping your foot low by trying to make a slight noise on the mat with that foot.) Here *tori* has just delivered the foot slap; the opponent's foot is forced up off the mat.

OKURI ASHI HARAI (SIDE SWEEPING ANKLE)

This foot sweep does not involve tremendous power, but depends on good timing and speed. You sweep your opponent's feet in the direction he is moving in and pull his torso in the opposite direction. Once again, this push-pull force will put your opponent on a horizontal plane.

It is a simple manoeuvre and can be used as an offensive move in itself or as a good follow through when another throw is blocked. In *okuri ashi harai* you can sweep from

c. Here you see just how effective *tori*'s arms are. He used his left hand to lift his opponent up and away from his feet. His right hand pulls him down and away from his feet. This striking foot continues to follow through, sweeping his opponent's feet clearly out from under him.

d. *Tori* has combined arm push-pull with a quick, hard foot slap to put his opponent onto the horizontal plane.

either side, using your right or left foot. Always slap your opponent's feet away from his body, striking with the sole of your foot.

Figure 17. In judo, force should be directed precisely. If a throw calls for the use of both arms, you cannot expect to throw an opponent using only one arm. Notice here the tension in the cloth of the *gi*; it will give you an idea how much pull *tori* exerts with his right arm. The other arm lifts the opponent up and off his feet.

Figure 18. *Kosoto gari* (minor outer reaping).
a. *Tori* has created a perfect opening for *kosoto gari* simply by manouevring his opponent on the mat. As his opponent steps forward with his left foot, *tori* steps to the side with his right foot. Now, at the very instant his opponent lifts his right foot to take a step forward, *tori* is ready to strike with his left foot. *Tori*'s left foot is slightly angled to the right, enabling him to get a good position for the strike.

b. *Tori* delivers the foot slap with his left foot, striking his opponent's heel with the sole of his foot. The slap should be low and hard. You should either try to make a slightly audible noise on the mat (as *tori* is doing here) or execute a short, powerful sweep upwards. The choice is yours, and it depends upon a fine point: if your opponent's foot is off the mat, sweep upwards – if it is firmly planted, sweep it along the mat.

KOSOTO GARI (MINOR OUTER REAPING)

By learning a relatively simple foot sweep such as *kosoto gari*, you can gain a deep and valuable insight into judo. To be able to react quickly, either defensively or offensively, a player must be relaxed and alert. If you are too tense, you can't feel what your opponent may do next.

Almost all beginners, many intermediate and a surprising number of top judo players simply try to overpower their opponents. This approach should be avoided; it may work for you in the local *dojo*, but ultimately will not be successful in a major *shiai*.

c. While *tori* has successfully followed through with his foot sweep, he has also used his arms very effectively to pull his opponent's torso backwards. His left arm exerts strong pressure on his opponent's right sleeve. His right arm pulls his opponent's lapel backward into a very awkward position.

d. *Tori* is putting his opponent into a horizontal position. With his legs out from under him, his torso pushed backward, the player falls to the mat.

You should play lightly until you see your opening, conserving your energy by not playing as hard as you can all the time. In so doing, you may also startle your opponent with a sudden show of power.

KOUCHI GARI (MINOR INNER REAPING)

If your timing isn't excellent, you will seldom succeed in performing *kouchi gari*. While the elements of the move itself are simple, the mastery of the timing takes time and practice. The figures illustrating this move show how *tori* catches *uke* off guard and then, with speed and force, hurls his entire body into the move. Once again, *kouchi gari* involves the basic principle of forcing an opponent's weight onto one leg, and then sweeping that leg out from under the opponent.

There are two excellent reasons for practising and mastering *kouchi gari*. Firstly, it is a good move in itself, but also it is a useful move for misleading your opponent with

Figure 19. *Kouchi gari* (minor inner reaping).
a. Here, *tori* has spotted a weakness in her opponent's defence. Her opponent has just put his foot down a little too far forward. His weight appears to be on the heel of that extremely vulnerable right foot. (You can also catch an unwary player when he's stepping backwards.)

b and c. With speed, *tori* pounces upon her opponent. She spins on her left foot and whips her right foot around, slapping it against her opponent's right heel. The more weight your opponent has going onto that heel, the more effective your strike will be. Simultaneously, *tori* is using her arms to upset her opponent's balance. Her right arm pushes back and then down. Her left arm pulls her opponent down towards the mat.

c

d

d. To succeed, you must follow through. With your right foot, you must bring your opponent's foot towards you. Similarly, you must follow through with your arms. As *tori*, you must commit yourself to the throw, striving with every motion to bring your opponent down.

initially, so that you can then follow up with a powerful hip throw.

Kouchi gari, being a minor throw, rarely gains an *ippon*. This being so, you should always be prepared to follow up your attack with a continuation throw if the opponent remains upright, or continue with ground work if he is knocked over.

Figure 20. *Ippon seoi nage* (single wing shoulder throw)
a. Look for the opportunity; your opponent may have a 'stiff' arm or may simply be leaning too far forwards. To create the opportunity, try to bait an opponent, by a push. A fraction of a second before he returns the push step in for the *ippon seoi nage.* At the same time, grab his sleeve with one hand and put the other under that same arm, as high up on his arm as you can get.
b. As you step – or some cases hop – in, you must pivot on your lead foot, and bring the other foot back between your opponent's legs. As you practise this entry, make the step, pivot and bend your knees, doing this in one movement.
c. Sometimes you have to slam into your opponent with your hips. In this throw, the trick is to come in low and then, once in position, straighten your legs and hips, making your opponent bounce up out of his position and eventually onto your back.
d. As soon as you pivot into position, slip your arm under your opponent's armpit and lock it with the crook of your elbow. The higher up you can get your arm, the tighter a grip you will have on your opponent. It is this arm lever, of course, which helps you get your opponent upon your back. If you

IPPON SEOI NAGE (SINGLE WING SHOULDER THROW)

For *ippon seoi nage* to be effective, a judo player has to execute the throw with speed and power, particularly speed. You have to be able to get 'inside' without making your intention obvious to your opponent, since *ippon seoi nage* can easily be blocked. Once 'inside', however, an experienced player will get his throw easily.

c

d

e

f

feel as though the throw is coming off your heels, you will not be getting the kind of power you need to throw somebody successfully. You must throw off your toes.

e and f. Once you have your opponent off his feet, it is a simple matter to drop him to the floor. With one hand you are pulling him onto your back; with the other you are pulling down and off. Under such pressure he will slam onto his back on the mat.

ERI SEOI NAGE (LAPEL SHOULDER THROW)

Eri seoi nage is a powerful weapon against a taller, heavier opponent, as it provides the smaller player with enormous leverage.

In *eri seoi nage* you aim to get your opponent on your back and then use both hands to throw him off and onto the mat. For the throw to be effective, the attacker must be low. It is far easier to get a person onto your back from a low position, and if you are shorter than your opponent you have that much more of an advantage over him.

Figure 21. *Eri seoi nage* (lapel shoulder throw).
a. *Tori* has a good right-hand grip on his opponent's lapel, which may be loose. *Tori*'s left hand has a good grip on his opponent's right sleeve.

b. *Tori* has stepped in with his right foot, the same way he would enter for an *ippon seoi nage*. Similarly, his left arm pulls his opponent's right arm out and up, unweighting his opponent. At this instant his right hand is twisting into his opponent's lapel.

c. As *tori* gets inside and low, he pivots, spinning on his right foot, and brings his left foot deep inside his opponent's legs. His hips are almost level with his opponent's knees.

d. The 'low' position is the key to successful *eri seoi nage*, as it allows a good hip lift and it also makes it easier to pull your opponent onto your back. Once he is on your back, he is completely vulnerable to the throw.

e. To throw his opponent, *tori* has done nothing more than straighten his legs and pull with both arms. With plenty of leverage in his arms and hips, he can easily get him onto his back.

f. Once you're into a throw, finish it off. In *eri seoi nage*, you simply pull as hard as you can, using both arms. If your opponent resists, you may be able to throw by dropping to one or both of your knees, which may force him to fall over you. Be sure to pull your opponent over your shoulder and straight down. If you throw him to the side, you'll weaken your throw.

While the footwork and the use of the hips are strikingly similar to that of an *ippon seoi nage*, you will be using your hands and arms in a completely different manner. As you pull his left sleeve with your right hand, your right hand *twists* into your opponent's lapels. That twisting motion allows you to pull really hard. Now, with your right hand twisting, pull that arm forwards. Your right elbow very naturally falls into the opponent's left armpit, and that provides you with a lot of leverage for the throw.

OGOSHI (MAJOR HIP THROW)

Many players find it difficult to use this throw on anyone but a beginner, who is likely to be completely open, disregarding his defensive position. However, *ogoshi* can be a unique weapon as a second throw. You might, for instance, try an *osoto gari*; your opponent could well immediately step back, and at that point he must be off balance. Or alternatively, he might try a move on you which fails, and at that point he would quite probably be off balance and susceptible to an *ogoshi*.

a

b

Figure 22. *Ogoshi* (major hip throw).
a. As in any hip throw, you lead with your right foot, placing it slightly ahead of your opponent's right foot. You pivot on that foot and bring your left foot deep inside your opponent's legs. In the photograph at left *tori* shows clearly how he reaches around his opponent's waist the second he steps in with that right foot. Simultaneously, he uses his left hand to bring his opponent's right arm up and out. This has the effect of 'unweighting' his opponent, making him easier to pick up and throw.
b. What is unweighting all about? At right, below, *tori* has pulled his opponent up with his left hand, pushing him up with his hips, all with the purpose of unweighting him from the mat. Once his opponent is unweighted, *tori* has a firm right arm around his waist and can roll him off his hips with ease. To get more lifting power with your legs, try to straighten them with a spring or snap.
c. Now with his opponent actually off his feet, *tori* prepares to throw him off his hips.
d. The opponent is thrown off *tori*'s right shoulder, over his hips and down in front of him.
e. His opponent hits the mat: *tori* remains on his feet, ready to slide into a hold-down choke or armlock if required.

Figure 23. *Harai goshi* (sweeping hip throw).
a. At left, *tori*, who can go to either side for an attack, decides to strike against his opponent's left side.

b. Having stepped forward with his striking foot *tori* pivots on it; b. shows the interplay of a co-ordinated arm-and-leg attack. *Tori*'s left arm is pulling his opponent forward.

HARAI GOSHI (SWEEPING HIP THROW)

This manoeuvre looks deceptively simple when you watch a black belt throw an opponent with this highly powerful hip throw. However, don't be fooled – *harai goshi* requires a combination of speed, strength, balance and excellent co-ordination. *Harai goshi* looks unstoppable, and is indeed a very hard throw to stop.

You need to practise hard with *harai goshi*. The key to this throw lies in steady practice of its opening steps. First, step slightly forwards with your left foot and pivot on that foot. Now, step back deeply with your right foot and place it in between your opponent's feet. The key is to step sufficiently deeply, for you will be balancing on that right foot, and for adequate power and balance, you should be on the ball of the foot. If you don't step deeply enough, you will not have a powerful platform for the throw and will feel as though you are being pulled backwards.

c. The footwork is critical in *harai goshi.* At left, *tori*'s left foot has completed the pivot and his right one is going deep between his opponent's legs.
d. Now *tori*'s other leg sweeps back against the opponent's left leg. The combination arm pull and leg sweep takes the opponent off his feet and onto *tori*'s hip. As the opponent rolls off *tori*'s hip (at centre), you can clearly see why that right foot (in a left-side attack) must be placed securely and properly. For an instant both men are balanced on *tori*'s right leg.
e. Using his arms, *tori* completes the throw by driving his opponent down onto the mat.

Once you have mastered the rhythm of the steps, practise the feeling of pulling your opponent towards you with your left arm. With your right arm, pull his left arm forwards. As with all hip lifting techniques, enter with your hips as low as comfort will allow.

PAT 50
SUE 15
KATHY 11

It is important to get a good grip on your opponent. Note here how *tori* has reached around *uke*'s neck to grab deeply onto his shoulder. The other hand will grip tightly onto *uke*'s arm for the powerful pull which pulls *uke* off balance forwards. Notice also how closely *tori* fits in against *uke*; as close as possible to provide the turning point.

Here we see two judo players getting good hard grips in a *randori*.

Figure 24. *Utsuri goshi* (changing hip throw).
a. *Uke* attempts to use *harai goshi* on *tori*. He steps in against *tori* and tries to grab him around his neck.
b. To block this throw, *tori* quickly sinks into a deep, defensive crouch and, just as *uke* attempts to get back into position, wraps his arms tightly around *uke*'s waist.

UTSURI GOSHI (CHANGING HIP THROW)

There are very many opportunities in judo for the player who prepares himself against the opponent's attack. Surprise can count as much as strength, and by executing an unexpected manoeuvre, a beginner might even defeat a black belt!

For example, you know that at some point your opponent will attempt an *uchi mata*, and *osoto gari* or a *harai goshi* against you. Surprise him with a countermove. For example, when a player attacks you with a *harai goshi*, you can block his attack successfully with a simple move. Throw your hips into his hips and jut them out ahead of your body. With timing, strength and the use of *utsuri goshi*, you can throw your opponent.

In figure 24, you can clearly see how *tori* has stopped *uke's harai goshi* and countered with a successful *utsuri goshi*.

c. Because he is in such a low position, *tori* can lift *uke* easily with his legs. In this position on *tori*'s hips *uke* is obviously vulnerable to *utsuri goshi.*
d. As he holds *uke* high on his hips, *tori* brings his left hip around to the right, switching the relative position of his opponent in mid air.

e. As *tori* moves his left hip around, he twists and drops *uke* onto that hip, still holding him tightly around the waist. He has put *uke* on a horizontal plane.
f. With his arms *tori* throws his opponent to the right, off that left hip. *Tori* completes *utsuri goshi* by throwing *uke* on his back for a clean point, an *ippon.*

Figure 25. *Hane goshi* (springing hip throw).
Tori makes an attack of *eri seoi nage*. *Uke* attempts to escape by pivoting on the toes of his left foot, and then *tori* converts to *hane goshi*.
a. Before you start *hane goshi*, you need to get a good tough grip with both hands. Grab as much of the material of your opponent's *gi* as you can. Here *tori* is throwing to his left. For a left-side *hane goshi*, your throwing hand grabs your opponent's collar; your right hand grasps his sleeve. Experienced judo players fight for their grips, and you should too.

HANE GOSHI (SPRINGING HIP THROW)

Hane goshi requires speed. In order to throw a player with this technique, you must move more quickly than average. As in all hip throws, you step in with one foot, pivot on that foot and bring the other foot deep inside your opponent's legs. In *hane goshi*, you whirl and spring inside your opponent's legs. Get your hips under your opponent's and lift first, then your bent leg brushes your opponent's out from under him. From that point onwards, you simply roll him off with your arms.

Springing quickly and accurately inside your opponent's legs takes practice. You can spring into the step and get a faster entry with *harai goshi*, *ippon seoi nage* and *koshi guruma*. The very fact that you are leaping into your throw will make your attack not only faster but also sharper and more directly focussed.

b. His spring complete, *tori* starts pulling his opponent onto his hips with his arms. Notice how *tori* bends that left leg slightly. With that bent leg, he is going to knock his opponent's left leg out from under him.
c. *Tori* slams into his opponent, pulling furiously with his arms to get his opponent onto his hips.
d. Merely by following through with his powerful spring, *tori* lifts his opponent up high, ready to drop him to the mat. It is worth remembering that you should try to lift your opponent with your hips and then turn him with your leg.

TSURI KOMI GOSHI (RESISTING HIP THROW)

This throw is designed to overcome an opponent's resistance against your hip attack. If you see that your opponent is too erect or is off his feet slightly, that is the time to attack with *tsuri komi goshi*. With this throw, you are trying to push him further off his feet, 'unweighting' him. Then you pull him onto your hips and throw him.

Tsuri komi goshi is a remarkably good counterthrow. When someone has tried an *osoto gari* and missed, he is especially vulnerable to *tsuri komi goshi*.

Figure 26. *Tsuri komi goshi* (resisting hip throw).
a. *Tori* steps inside with his right foot, pivoting on that foot, and simultaneously grabs a lot of his opponent's collar with his right hand. He takes a firm grip on the collar because he'll be lifting his opponent up with that hand.
b. As *tori* comes in, his hips are low. As he pulls his opponent onto his hips, he'll straighten his legs to give himself extra lifting power. Notice how powerfully his left hand and arm are pulling his opponent's right arm out and up. *Tori*'s right hand virtually straight arms his opponent's neck, pushing him upward. This is the most distinctive aspect of the throw.

c. With his right hand pushing his opponent up, *tori* has put his hips solidly into his opponent's legs. He is ready to throw.
d and e. To throw him over his hips, *tori* now pulls with both arms. The result is a clean fall.

Figure 27. *Sode tsuri komi goshi* (sleeve resisting hip throw).
Uke tries a standing cross strangle. *Tori* forces the attacking arm high into the air, as he turns his hips in to the counter attack with *sode tsuri komi goshi.*
a. First you must twist away from your opponent's choke. At the same time, bring your arm under his choking arm and grab his elbow.
b. Next, bring your left foot around behind you and place it between your opponent's legs. Because *sode tsuri komi goshi* is a hip throw, the footwork will be the same as for an *ogoshi* or a *harai goshi.*

SODE TSURI KOMI GOSHI (SLEEVE RESISTING HIP THROW)

The difference between this and the previous throw is that in *tsuri goshi* you lift an opponent by the collar; in *sode tsuri kome goshi*, you lift him by the sleeve. It is also a very good counterthrow.

Your opponent may quickly move in on you, attempting to choke you while you are both standing up. This is easy to counter, as you will see in figure 27.

c. Pushing mightily on your opponent's choking arm, throw him over your back. At this point, your left hand should be pulling on your opponent's other arm.
d and e. In one fluid movement, pull your opponent across your back.

UCHI MATA (INNER THIGH THROW)

Uchi mata is a classic throw, involving the utmost in speed, co-ordination and power, all released at the same moment. To sense the opportunity for such a throw and to execute it well requires concentration and clarity of thought.

Experienced players find that *uchi mata* is a very effective form of attack when the opponent is standing defensively with the legs wide apart. It can also be very effective against a taller opponent.

Figure 28. *Uchi mata* (inner thigh throw).
a. Sensing that his opponent is vulnerable, *tori* picks up his left foot to start his *uchi mata*.

b. *Tori* is pivoting on his right foot as he brings his left foot around. Now he will thrust it deep between his opponent's legs as he hops back with his right foot. Some players step; *tori* hops because he believes it adds speed to his move.

c. You must get deep inside his legs to avoid striking him in the groin. Judo is a sport, and at no time must you risk injuring another player. Note in this sequence how *tori* brings his opponent's weight on to the leg he is about to attack.

d. Deep inside and under his opponent, a position which is critical to the success of the throw, *tori* pulls his opponent onto his hip with his arms. Now he straig-htens out that left foot (the one between his opponent's thighs) in order to sweep it up against his opponent.

e. *Tori* is actually bouncing his opponent onto his hip and then twisting him off and over onto the mat. As the opponent starts to fall, *tori*'s concentration is unbroken. He aims his forehead at the mat.

f. Once his opponent is airborne, *tori* completes twisting him off his hip and drops him to the mat.

Figure 29. *Soto makikomi* (outer winding).
a. As *tori* makes his initial move in, his opponent may expect a *harai goshi*. Accordingly, the opponent may brace himself, with his arm stiff and his hips thrust toward the front, to block that throw.
b. *Tori* pulls with great force against the opponent's right arm. With the other arm, he is planning to trap his opponent's right shoulder as high as possible. He pivots in order to thrust his left hip into the right hip of the opponent.

SOTO MAKIKOMI (OUTER WINDING)

Many judo players use a stiff arm to keep opponents from getting in close. *Soto makikomi* is a formidable weapon in such a situation; it is also a good throw to use as a follow up to an *osoto gari* or a *harai goshi* which you have tried but which your opponent has effectively blocked. In this case, you don't return to your original position but switch in mid-action to *soto makikomi*. In effect, you wind yourself up in your opponent's body and simultaneously throw yourself at the mat. You should hit the mat on your shoulder. If you don't do the throw correctly, however, you'll hit the mat with your head, so take care!

When practising *soto makikomi* be sure that your partner is a very safe player with considerable expertise in falling, for it takes a clever player to fall well from this throw.

c. *Tori* stretches out his right arm, enabling him to get a high position on his opponent's shoulder. At this point his entire body is thrust back tightly against his opponent's.
d. Once *tori* gets his shoulder and hip position, he throws himself into a roll toward the mat. He is aiming his right shoulder at the mat. His opponent is being thrown, and because of the snapping motion, he will hit the mat hard.

e. Notice that *tori*'s opponent breaks the major force of the fall by a perfectly timed mat slap.

TAI OTOSHI (BODY DROP)

This throw exemplifies the entire spirit of judo; the gentle use of force, the meticulous sense of timing, and the clever use of another person's strength. *Tai otoshi* in particular demands good timing and co-ordination rather than strength.

First of all, it can be executed quickly, with little more than a pivot. No steps are needed, so it is a fast and effective move against someone who, for a second, might be caught leaning forwards. It is also a good move against a taller, heavier opponent because against a smaller player the taller, heavier player has to bend over or lean forward, leaving himself open for *tai otoshi*.

Figure 30. *Tai otoshi* (body drop).
a. *Tori* has stepped slightly forward with his right foot, pivoting on that foot and bringing his left foot around and behind him. His left foot must be just outside and in front of his opponent's left foot, so that he will be able to get a good leverage for the throw.

In this throw you either make your opponent put his weight on one foot, then step across his legs with the other one, or push his torso onto that one foot and pull him forwards across your outstretched leg. In other words, you trip him. *Tai otoshi* comes into the *te waza* or hand throw group of throws, the power of the throw in this case coming from the hands and shoulders.

b. With his right foot *tori* steps across his opponent's right foot. As he steps his right arm pushes against his opponent's neck, driving him to the right. Simultaneously, *tori*'s left arm is pulling his opponent forward, over *tori*'s outstretched right leg. Notice how his right knee is bent; it is the trigger for the throw.
c. *Tori* has held that key right leg as straight as a ramrod. His opponent's body is now forced to tumble over *tori*'s leg.
d and e. The combination of *tori*'s timing, speed and such precise use of force overpowers his opponent instantaneously.

TOMOE NAGE (STOMACH THROW)

Tomoe nage demonstrates how you may give way to an opponent's aggressive pushing. You have probably seen this throw a hundred times, in films, on television or even on the stage. It is a spectacular throw; suddenly one player is thrown high over the other's head, seemingly without effort.

In *tomoe nage*, you sacrifice your upright position for a horizontal attacking position. The throw is designed to take overwhelming advantage of a person who rushes in to attack you. As he presses in at you, you step closer to him, grab the lapel deeply and fall onto your back, placing one of your feet securely in the pit of your opponent's stomach. As you fall, pull hard on his lapels and simultaneously push your foot against his stomach. Straighten out your leg, and as you push with your foot and pull down on his lapels he will go flying over your shoulder and land resoundingly on his back.

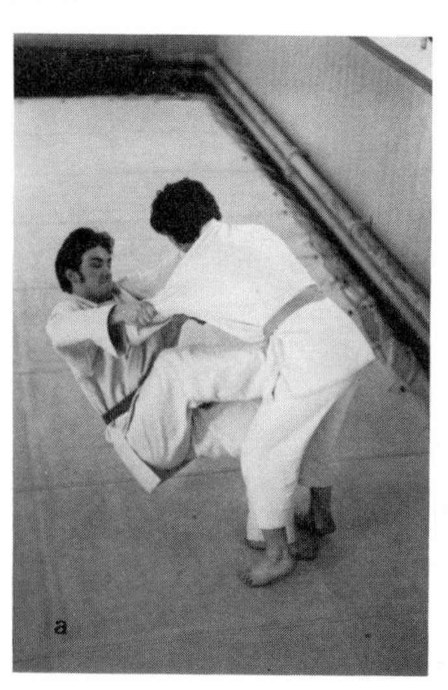
a

b

It is a perfect throw for a small person to use against a heavier, taller opponent. It is also a good throw to use when your opponent is in deep defensive crouch, as it enables you to go in and under him.

Figure 31. *Tomoe nage* (stomach throw).
a. As your opponent rushes at you, step in toward him. Your left foot should be between your opponent's legs. Swing your right foot out and up in preparation for implanting it in his stomach. You should have a good, solid grip on your opponent's lapels.
b. Now you fall backwards onto the mat. Pull strongly on his lapels, but do not exert pressure on his stomach yet. If you push with your foot too soon, you will block the throw, because your foot pressure will keep him up.
c. As you land on your back on the mat, your opponent should be directly over you. Now – and only now – thrust your leg out powerfully and quickly. That will propel him into a complete somersault. Aim to throw him over one shoulder. Here *tori* is throwing his opponent over his left shoulder, so he maintains that pulling pressure with the left hand and lets go with his right.
d. With a successful *tomoe nage*, you'll throw your opponent some distance. Cleanly executed, it is spectacular to watch and extremely satisfying to the player. Like many throws in judo, *tomoe nage* is an excellent self-defence throw.

4 Hold-down Techniques (Osae Komi Waza)

At least half of judo is played on the ground, wrestling with an opponent using hold-downs, armlocks and chokes. Mentally, mat work is as stimulating as the throwing techniques. The purpose of the ground techniques is simple enough – you try to control your opponent's body for a certain length of time, or make him give up by tapping the mat or saying *mattai* meaning 'enough'. You can win by using hold-downs, or making your opponent capitulate by a choke or armlock.

In a hold-down you win by holding your opponent down for thirty seconds (see pp. 27). Once you get a legitimate hold-down, the referee says '*Osae komi*', indicating that the timekeeper has started counting the seconds. If your opponent then breaks the hold-down,the referee says '*Osae komi toketa*', meaning that the hold has been broken.

Judo is best seen as a continuous flow of action in which you seek by throw, choke, armlock or ground hold-down to control your opponent. Thinking of the sport in this way will help you to understand *osae komi waza*, the hold-downs. You can actually start thinking of a hold-down during the throw itself. If your opponent has thrown you poorly, it may be possible for you to turn and get a good hold-down on him the minute you hit the mat. Of course, when you throw an opponent, he will end up on his back, which provides the perfect opportunity for any number of ground work attacks.

In attacking someone or defending yourself, you should

obviously keep your body low and your weight evenly distributed. Flexibility counts, too, for if you are too rigid you won't be able to move quickly.

You might find it helpful to think in terms of mechanics, again. You are using leverage to break your opponent's leverage. If he is trying to arch his back, get control of his head by trying to get under his neck and lifting it off the mat. He won't have any leverage then. Or try to get control of his arms or legs; the idea is to prevent the opponent from getting the leverage he needs by controlling the part of the body used to gain it.

Flexibility is also essential in mastering *osae komi waza*. You must be able to shift your weight from one part of your opponent's body to another as he changes his defence. Your aim is to remain in control by constantly shifting, using your strength to its maximum and trying to prevent your opponent from using his maximum strength.

KESA GATAME (SCARF HOLD DOWN)

Kesa gatame is the most common of all judo holds. Although mastering it takes time and practice, it is easy to learn and remarkably easy to use. Once mastered, *kesa gatame* becomes a formidable weapon.

You must expect several reactions from your opponent. He may try to push your head up and away with his free left arm. If he does, bend your head down and to the outside. He may also try to hook your left leg with his right leg. To stop him doing this, just keep moving him in a clockwise pattern.

If you think he is going to break your grip, you can lock your hands together. But you do this at your own risk because it is a good opportunity for your opponent to escape. The person escaping will swing both his legs from side to side, creating enough force to unseat you. At the same time, he will probably grab your belt in the back and pull you onto his hip. Now, if your hands are locked together your opponent will push his head against the mat, trapping your hand there. When he rocks, you will not be able to brace against that motion, and he could escape.

Figure 32. *Kesa gatame* (scarf hold down).
Tori threw his opponent with an *osoto gari* a second or two before this photography was taken. He then took advantage of the fact that his opponent was more or less on his back by simply moving quickly into his opponent's right side to *kesa gatame.*
Tori sits close to the right side of his opponent. He gains tremendous stability by spreading his legs out, keeping them slightly bent for even greater strength.
With his right hand, he has reached around his opponent's collar as far as possible. He hasn't grabbed the collar, but keeps his hand flat on the mat and applies pressure against the back of his opponent's head with his forearm.
Tori's left arm traps his opponent's right arm. To make his trap effective, he takes a lot of material from the upper sleeve of his opponent's *gi.* Note especially how he not only grips strongly but pulls the arm up, stretching it out and reducing its effectiveness.
Bend your head down as low as you need to. Your opponent may push at your head or chin with his free left forearm. Keeping your head low will help deflect the force of such pushes.
Try to think heavy. This isn't as ridiculous as it sounds. Concentrate on keeping your whole body low; it makes it a lot more difficult for your opponent.

KAMI SHIHO GATAME (UPPER FORE QUARTER HOLDING)

When your instructor first shows you how to execute *kami shiho gatame*, you will wonder how you could use such a hold on anyone. It certainly looks difficult, but you will find many opportunities to use it.

For instance, suppose someone had gained a *waza ari* over you with a partially successful *tomoe nage*, you could, if you turned around quickly enough, work into *kami shiho gatame*. Of course, you always work into a hold, for no one is going to lie there waiting for you. Work first with one hand, then the other, confuse your opponent by attempting a choke, then move in quickly with this hold.

Suppose you have been thrown and are now scrambling fast to lie on top of your opponent. First, work one of your arms under his arm, trapping it against his side. Hook the thumb of that arm into your opponent's belt, and then work the other arm under his remaining arm, also hooking your thumb into his belt.

When you have trapped his arms, think of yourself as a heavy weight pressing into your opponent. Your chin presses into his stomach, your chest against his shoulders. You can straddle his head between your legs. For greater stability, stretch your legs out wide on the floor.

KATA GATAME (SHOULDER HOLDING)

This is one of the strongest holds in judo. Not only is the player completely immobile, but he can also be choked into submitting with *kata gatame*.

It is hard to get this hold, of course, but the opportunity will present itself when you are holding a judo player with *kesa gatame* and he tries to elbow you or push your head away from him. As he brings that arm up across his body, release your *kesa gatame*, reach behind his outstretched arm with one hand and lock hands. Squeeze his arm into his neck; he will inevitably submit. This is a simple and very effective move.

Figure 33. *Kami shiho gatame* (upper fore quarter holding).
a. Shows the hold-down with *tori* straddling his opponent's head.
b. *Tori* stretches out his legs for greater stability against the twisting and turning of the man underneath. Either way you choose, you trap your opponent's arms against his sides, hooking your thumbs into his belt, and then press down with your body.

Figure 34. *Kata gatame* (shoulder holding).
a. As you squeeze and pull your arm together, put your head to the floor. This helps increase the pressure on your opponent.

b. As you get in for *kata gatame*, twist your knee in against your opponent's side to prevent him from getting away.

YOKO SHIHO GATAME (SIDE FORE QUARTERS HOLDING)

This is quite a simple hold. Anyone who has ever wrestled will recognise it as a good position for pinning the opponent. In judo, of course, you don't have to pin someone, you need only control him by keeping him on his back.

Figure 35. *Yoko shiho gatame* (side fore quarter holding).
With *yoko shiho gatame*, you move in from the side at a right angle. Next, press your chest against his stomach, thinking of yourself as a heavy weight. With your right hand, reach between his legs and try to grab his belt from underneath. With your left hand, reach in and grab his collar, holding it firmly. Bring your right knee in against his waist. This will prevent him from twisting in toward you in an effort to escape. As he twists away from you, you can use your head to prevent yourself from being rolled. Or you can momentarily release your left hand from his collar to brace yourself against a roll.

5 Choking Techniques (Shime Waza)

At first, the thought of choking or being choked, makes beginners rather apprehensive. However, it is a natural and useful element of judo, and is used in conjunction with throws and hold-downs. A judo choke is pressure against the carotid artery, the jugular vein or the windpipe, or all three. In fact, to be strictly accurate, attacks against the windpipe are chokes, and attacks against the carotid artery and jugular vein are strangleholds, but here it will be useful to describe them all together.

To win by choking, you must make your opponent submit with his hands or feet, or call out 'submit'. You must be well aware of his condition when you are performing these movements, for he can actually lose consciousness or lack the freedom of movement to tap unless you are careful.

To apply a choke, you must move fast, getting your grip without being too obvious about it, and choke quickly and strongly. You should have complete control over your opponent so he is unable to break away.

As you gain experience, you will instinctively look for opportunities in which to use the choke or in which you can distract your opponent by attemping a choke and then going on to another strategy.

A word of warning: you *must* release your opponent instantly at the signal of surrender.

ESCAPING FROM A CHOKE

The best way to escape from a choke is to keep your chin down, guarding your neck from a stranglehold. Don't let yourself fall into a vulnerable position. In certain cases, you can use your arms to push or twist away from the elbow of your opponent's choking arm.

GYAKU JUJI JIME (REVERSE CROSS NECKLOCK)

It can be an advantage to be on the bottom in judo, particularly when you can apply *gyaku juji jime*. It is a fundamental choke, one that is used quite often. It consists of reaching deep inside your opponent's collar with crossed hands, then applying pressure against the sides of his neck.

Figure 36. *Gyaku juji jime* (reverse cross necklock).
a. Work your right hand in deep on your opponent's right collar, in grabbing position, with your fingers inside and your thumb on the outside. Your left hand should be in equally deep on your opponent's left collar.
b. To choke your opponent, simply bring your hands together and bring him down on your chest. If you are on top of your opponent, lean over his head; it makes the choke more effective.

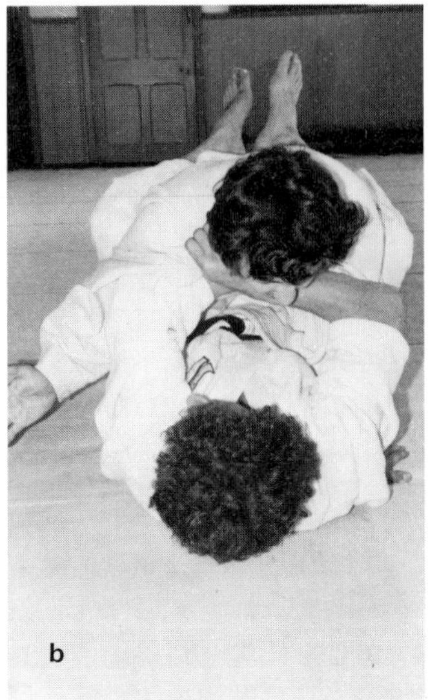

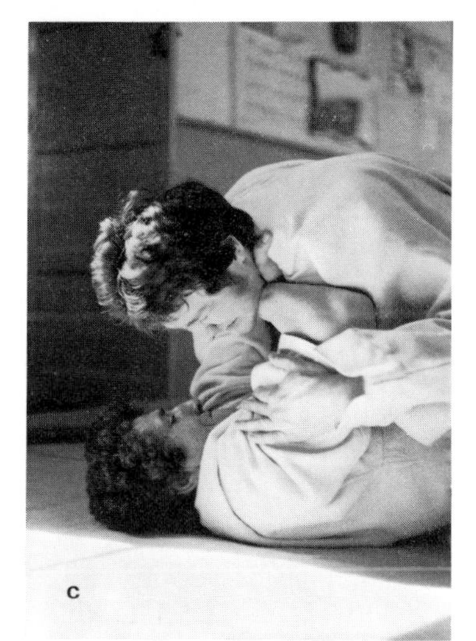

Figure 37. Kata juji jime (half cross necklock).
a. See how the positions of the hands are reversed – left thumb out, right thumb in.
b. *Tori* goes deep before twisting his opponent's left collar for the choke.
c. *Tori* pulls his opponent down onto his chest; he uses his legs to prevent his opponent from rolling or twisting away from the choke.

KATA JUJI JIME (HALF CROSS NECKLOCK)

The *kata* choke is a minor variation of *gyaku*, the basic cross choke. It, too, can be used either when your opponent is on top or when you are on top.

Let us assume that you are underneath your opponent. Move quickly to grab his left collar with your left hand, placing your thumb on the outside of the lapel. Be sure you get deep enough inside the collar or you won't have enough leverage to do the choking. With your right hand, cross over and grab his right lapel, with your thumb on the inside and the fingers outside.

The choking action takes place when you twist your left hand so that the thumb on the outside of the lapel now touches your opponent's neck. Pull him towards you with your right hand. If the squeezing action is at all effective, your opponent will become uncomfortable immediately and will undoubtedly submit.

HADAKA JIME (NAKED NECKLOCK)

Once you get this choke on an opponent, he is not going to break it easily. If he is careless enough to let you move in on him from the rear, quickly place your right hand across his throat before he realises what is going on.

OKURI ERI JIME (SLIDING COLLAR NECKLOCK)

Okuri eri jime is simple, very strong and relatively easy to apply in a variety of positions.

One hand slides across your opponent's throat and locks onto the lapel of the *gi* – your thumb will be inside. Your other hand goes underneath his other arm and pulls down on his opposite collar. So one hand chokes by putting the thin edge of your wrist against his throat and the other traps him in that position by maintaining pressure on the other lapel of the *gi*.

If you are lying down, wrap your legs around his waist and stretch backwards. This will stretch his body out,

Figure 38. *Hadaka jime* (naked necklock).
You have to get your right hand across before he starts to defend his throat by bringing his chin down. Then reach over his left shoulder with your left hand. Lock both palms together and pull back against your opponent's throat.

This is a variation of *hadaka jime*. You simply use your arms a bit differently to achieve the choke. Your right arm still slides in front of your opponent's throat, but the difference is that your left arm is positioned on your opponent's left shoulder, locking your right hand in your left elbow. Your left hand pushes against your opponent's head. This lock creates powerful leverage, making this variation even more devastating than the basic *hadaka jime*.

making it just about impossible for him to escape

The best opportunity for *okeri eri jime* comes when you and your opponent are kneeling side by side on the mat. It happens very often. Put your hands in the choking position and sit down. From this position, *okeri eri jime* can be very effective, and catches many opponents unawares.

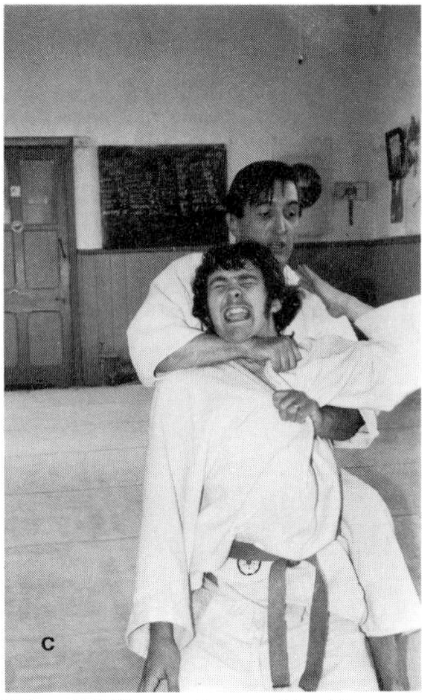

Figure 39. *Okuri eri jime* (sliding collar necklock).
a and b. Notice that the thumb of the choking hand is on the inside. The other hand goes under the opponent's arm and takes hold of the opposite lapel.
c. The pressure's on.

6 Armlock Techniques (Kansetu Waza)

Armlocks are excellent moves to use in self defence. As with hold-down techniques, armlocks involve the principles of leverage, and are used to follow upon other judo techniques. For instance, there is one armlock to be used after a throw and another to be used when a player lunges at you.

Kansetu waza are techniques of applying pressure to the elbow; the main idea is to gain complete control over your opponent's arm and force submission. However, to prevent injuries to the elbow, pressure should be applied with care.

If you are attacked with an armlock, you should either escape or submit quickly to avoid any chance of injury. With experience, players learn how much they can take before having to submit.

WAKI GATAME

You must always look for an opportunity to use *waki gatame*. If your opponent approaches you with one arm outstretched, he could be vulnerable to such an attack. It is a surprise move, which few players expect.

UDE GATAME (ARMLOCK WITH THE HANDS)

A straight armlock such as *ude gatame* can be applied in a variety of positions. It requires great speed. You grab your opponent's wrist, pull it out straight, twist it and apply pressure against his elbow. Be careful when you practise this, for a mistake is painful.

Figure 40. *Waki gatame.*
Pull your opponent's arm sharply toward you, stepping around to the side. Put one arm under the elbow of your opponent; put the other hand on the wrist of the exposed arm. Next, lock your free hand into his wrist. You now have the leverage to bend your opponent's arm against his elbow, a painful manoeuvre which automatically ends the point. Few judo players will risk injury by holding out, for it would be foolish. By holding *tori* is exerting pressure here, and his opponent is already submitting.

JUJI GATAME (CROSS ARMLOCK)

The figures below illustrate the 'flow' of judo well; you can see how you can move from a throw to an offensive attack on the mat. By following your opponent down quickly you can then go into an armlock, choke or hold-down.

Figure 42. *Juji gatame* (cross armlock).
a. The player has held onto the right wrist of the man he has just thrown. He then pulls up hard on his opponent's arm.
b. He sits down suddenly, as close as he can to his opponent's shoulder. With his left foot he steps over his opponent's head.
c. Now, he leans back on the mat, squeezing his opponent's elbow between his knees. In order to apply pressure, he arches back and twists the opponent's arm in the direction of the little finger of that hand.

Figure 41 (opposite). *Ude gatame* (armlock with the hands).
The key is to keep your opponent's arm outstetched. Then take his elbow with both hands, exerting pressure in towards your own body. You can prevent your opponent from rolling inwards by keeping one knee on his body. The armlock itself will prevent him from rolling away from you.

New Developments

At the time of reprinting, a number of changes are being considered by the major associations. The ultimate aim of these changes would be to return western judo to the original Japanese style. All of the following points are being discussed at present:

Jigo tai Fighting from a defended deep crouched stance currently used, is now considered by leading minds of the major associations to be detrimental to the spirit of judo. A solution would be to allow *jigo tai* only as an immediate means of defence to block or negate an attack.

Ne waza A return to the Japanese style would mean that entry into groundwork would be restricted to an attack that is considered sufficiently skilful to score *waza-ari*, or by natural falldown of one or both fighters during the course of the contest.

Koka/Yuko The British Judo Association are phasing out the *koka/yuko* scoring system and have discontinued them in their promotional examinations and junior grade competitions. The system is also being reviewed by the Amateur Judo Association and the British Judo Council (working under the IJF guidelines). The International Martial Arts Federation (Judo Division) who follow the teaching of and are governed by the International Martial Arts Academy of Japan do not train their members to the *koka/yuko* system.

7 Useful information

ADDRESSES

The International Martial Arts Federation (Headquarters in Great Britain)
87 Main Street
Seamer
nr Scarborough
Yorks YO12 4RF

British Schools Judo Association
Springfield
Old Sticklepatt Hill
Barnstaple EX31 2BG
Devon

British Judo Association
70 Brompton Road
London SW3 1DR

Scottish Judo Federation
8 Frederick St
Edinburgh EH2 2EY

Hibernia Judo Association
17 Chesterton House
Ingrave St
London SW11 2UD

Amateur Judo Association (British Headquarters)
98 Ardmory Avenue
Tory Glen
Glasgow

British Judo Council (British Headquarters)
21 Lowfield Road
Acton
London W3

BOOK LIST

All About Judo by Geoff Gleeson (E P Publishing)
Better Judo by Geoff Gleeson (Kaye and Ward)
Judo: Know the Game by the British Judo Association (E P Publishing)
Judo by Brian Jacks (Pelham)
The Complete Seven Katas of Judo by M. Kawaishi (Foulsham)

Glossary

CHUI Penalty of five points
DO Way or path
DOJO A place to practise judo
ERI Collar or lapel
GATAME Holding technique used in ground work
GI Clothing worn by judo players
HAJIME Begin (said by referee)
HAN SOKU MAKE Penalty of 10 points, meaning disqualification
HANTEI Judge's decision
HIKI WAKE A drawn contest
IPPON A score to the value of ten points
JIGO TAI Defensive stance
JU Gentle
JUDOKA One who practises judo
JUJITSU Ancient technique of self defence
KANSETU WAZA Armlock techniques
KATA Formal technique
KATAME WAZA Grappling techniques
KEI KOKU Penalty of seven points
KOKO A score to the value of three points
KUZUSHI The point at which the opponent's balance is completely broken
MA Straight
MATTAI Signal of submission
MATTE Stop
NAGE WAZA Throwing techniques

OBI Belt
OSAE KOMI Holding (controlling)
OSAE KOMI TOKETA A hold is broken
OSAE KOMI WAZA Holding techniques
RANDORI Fighting practice
REI A bow
SENSEI Instructor, usually 4th Dan, or above
SHIAI Contest
SHIDO Penalty of three points
SHIME WAZA Choking techniques
SHIZEN TAI Offensive stance
SODE Sleeve
SONO MAMA Freeze (stay as you are) a term used by the referee
SORE MADE That is all (said by referee)
SUMI Corner
TACHI REI Standing bow
TATAMI Judo mat
TE Hand
TOKETA Hold broken
TSUKURI Breaking an opponent's balance
UCHI Inner
UCHIKOMI Form practice
URA Rear
UDE Arm
UKEMI Falling technique
WAZA Techniques
WAZI ARI Score to the value of seven points
YOKO Side
YOSHI Continue (said by referee)
YUKO Score to the value of five points
YUSEGACHI Win by superiority, a decision in favour of
ZA REI Bow from sitting position

Index